T0313041

Seasons of the River

Poems by Dan Jaffe

Color Photos by Bob Barrett

Additional Photos by Lydia Swartz

BkMk PRESS-UMKC
College of Arts & Sciences
University of Missouri-Kansas City
5216 Rockhill Rd., Rm. 204
Kansas City, MO 64110-2499

ACKNOWLEDGEMENTS

"All the Seasons Pour into One River," has been set to music by Gerald Kemner and performed by the University of Missouri-Kansas City Chorale under the direction of Eph Ely.

"Seasons of the River: The River Dance," was part of a show of paintings and poems displayed at the Kansas City Jewish Community Center.

"River Behind the City," was the winner of the Kansas City Arts Commission Poetry Prize for a poem about Kansas City by a Kansas City poet, 1977. It later appeared in *The Kansas City Star*.

"On the Paseo Bridge," was runner up in the Kansas City Arts Commission competition.

Grateful appreciation to Kathy Sherman Boutros, Special Collections Librarian, Snyder Collection of Americana, General Library, UMKC; and to Paul L. Hilpmen, Prof. of Geosciences; also to Robert Stewart, and Pat Shields for editorial assistance.

Typography & Design Consultation by Michael Annis. Cover Design by Wayne Pycior. Printing by Walsworth (Marceline, MO).

George Catlin, *Buffalo Herds Crossing the Upper Missouri,* 1838, reproduced courtesy of & permission of Office of Research Support, National Museum of American Art, Smithsonian Institution, Washington, D.C. 20560. Gift of Mrs. Joseph Harrison, Jr.

Maps reproduced from *The Missouri River & Its Utmost Source* by J.V. Brower, 1897, Pioneer Press, St. Paul, Minn.; and *The Kansas City Bridge* by O. Chanute & George Morrison, 1870, D. Van Nostrad, N.Y.

A Mandan Village, reproduced from *The United States Illustrated*, ed. Charles Dana, 1853.

"Snags in the Missouri River," from *History of Early Steamboat Navigation on the Missouri River*, vol. I, edited by Hiram Martin Chittendon, 1903, Francis P. Harper.

"Steamboat Wreck on the Missouri River," from *History of Early Steamboat Navigation on the Missouri River,* vol. II.

Library of Congress Cataloging-in-Publication Data

Jaffe, Dan.
    Seasons of the river.

    1. Missouri River—Poetry. 2. Rivers—Poetry.
I. Barrett, Bob. II. Title.
PS3560.A3S4 1987 811'.54 86-71748
ISBN 0-933532-58-X

missouri arts council

Financial assistance for this project was provided by The Missouri Arts Council, a state agency.

The Literary Advisory Committee of the Council recommended the Arts Council provide funds to make possible publication of this book.

In memory of
Samuel Herbert Jaffe
and
John Anthony Ciardi

POEMS

PHOTOGRAPHS & ILLUSTRATIONS

COLOR PHOTOS

What Are You Looking For?

What are you looking for?
A snake falling out of the sky?
A face fashioned in the mountains?

No.   There's no need.

What then?   This is no Kingdom of Quivira.

So what?   It doesn't matter.

Then what do you keep looking for?

A place where four winds make one voice.
A place where one voice has many meanings.

That's a riddle I can't answer.

Listen to the May apples, to the yellow buds,
to the thistles and foxtails.
Listen to the sandstone and the mimosa,
to the wavering water and the murmurs of rust.

Why not look for one spot?
One actual spot?

Choose.

Find me a place out of time.
Then I'll choose.

Just look around.
Look at your own footprints.
Feel the horizon's still swirl.
Here behind the half-deserted airport,
at the backside of the city,
at the edge of two states
whose rivers merge,
from this center you can,
like the point of a compass,
turn through the seasons.

From the Great Bend

Climb up the bluffs
& find the wide view again.
History means stopping
the world and looking
at where you've been:

Out across Kersey Coates Drive,
over the railroad yards of the West Bottoms,
to the Great Bend of the Missouri,
that arc of water that set a city
at the crossing of a continent.

Along that sweep of river
old Joe Peppard, dealer in buffalo bones,
broadcast hybrid seed
from the Town of Kansas
wholesale to the world.

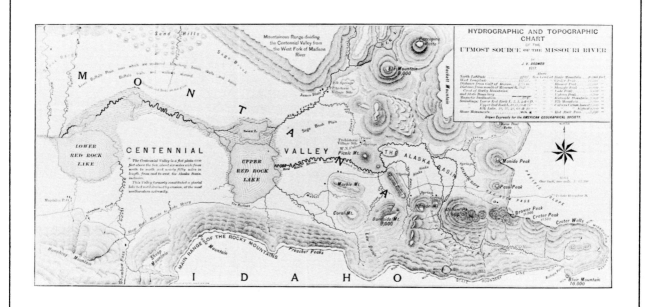

SEASONS OF THE RIVER

The River Dance:

Start in the sky.
Start with shapes of men
already in the clouds.
Start with tongue stirrings of lightning
        with mutters of thunder.

What falls,
shuffled by wind,
is clear voice,
whisper without words.

Go back.
Go back to the beginning of river.
Go back to the beginning time.
Always creation again.

Let us sip the droplets of the icicle,
        kiss the snowflake.

Earth collects sky
    in mountain pools,
    in basins of life.
The land drinks and stirs.
Under the drenched boulder
the land drinks and stirs.

Let there be a coming together.
Let the vowels of the fir and saxifrage commingle.
Let wet leaves gather into humus.
Let the streams grow, the land flower,
the wary eye of the raccoon
measure all things between his paws.
Let beaver and snake sing
their parts pure.

The river is history.
The river is a history of boulders shouldered by titans,
sanded by the wash of waters
into pebbles stippled as trout.
This upland stream has a jeweled bottom.

All one needs is a turtle's eye.

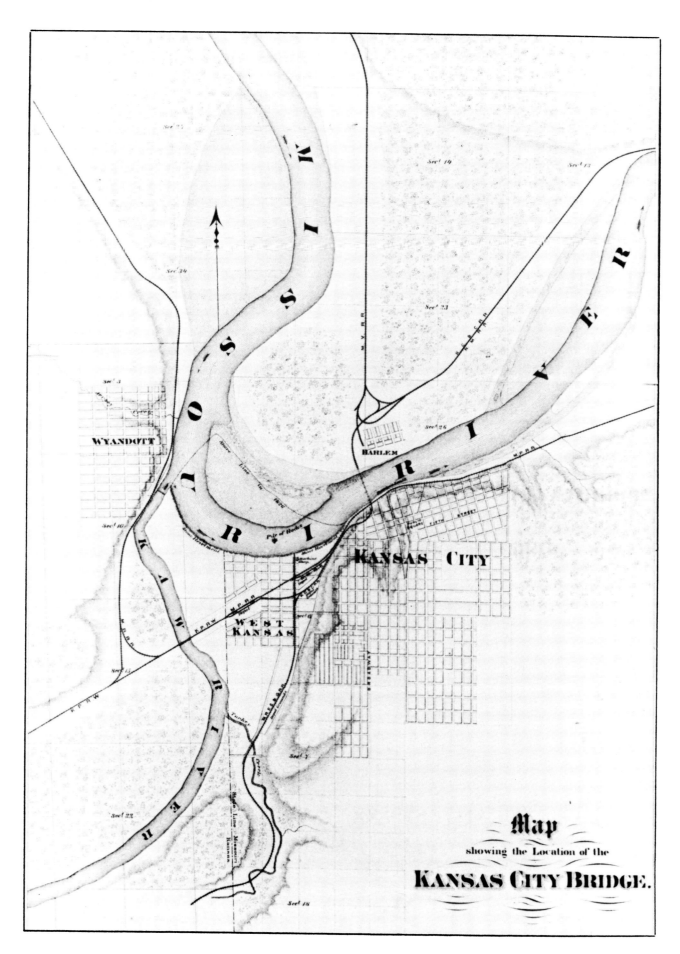

Map

showing the Location of the

KANSAS CITY BRIDGE.

The Map Is Not the River

The map is not the river.
No sudden currents upset the cartographer's pen.

The letters of this name: *Missouri:*
drape across the stylized landscape
like a patriotic banner.
But the map is not the river.

The river does not need a flag to run,
man to chart its curves,
to insinuate its course across the ridge line.
Man's history is not the river's.

Because his origins were eastward
& his route was west
this mapmaker found the Mississippi first,
thought it greater, confusing
wider with longer, first found
for true "Father of Waters."

He thinks he knows; therefore he names,
& his naming shows what he thinks is so.
The river neither notices nor cares.

The map is not the river.
No rising water floods the reader's eye.
One can scan the map in moments.
You cannot read this river in a lifetime.

The Water Prayer

High on his stallion
the Rain God herds clouds,
the children of the wind,
from the Rockies, from the Tetons,
wrings out their water.

Mighty Spirit who revives the dead,
Your power saves.
From heaven's well you send us rain,
send us water.
Water is your spirit.
Its drops revive, refresh.
And as we drink
we praise your power,
the power of water.

Through the desert, Your prophet
follows You like water.
You bless the holy like a tree
near a stream of water.
Your warrior You save
from fire and water.
We are the planters
of Your seed
near Rivers of water.

Do not refuse us in our dry times.
For the greatness of Your spirit
grant us abundant water.

Soften the earth with water.
Do not hold back.

Remember the births foretold by the rain,
the promises of thunder.
Remember how we pour out
our hearts like water.
Remember how deep our wells go.

Do not hold back.
Grant us abundant water.

We have dared the wilderness,
forded torrents,
risked white water.
We have wrestled
with the powers of fire and water.

Be with us again.
Come Rain, Come Rain.
Grant us abundant water.

We have dreamed of a shaman
rising from the river,
of a gourd tilted,
from under a boulder
a rivulet of water.

Remember the priest alone
by the river,
how he sprinkled water on ashes,
cleansing his people,
how they kept him away,
that people turbulent as water.
For his sake
grant us abundant water.

Remember the tribes
brought across many rivers,
how you sweetened for them the bitterness of waters,
how the blood of their sons spilled.
And remember how we too are like islands,
how enemies surround us like water.
Remember the tribes
and grant us abundant water.

Oh Mighty Spirit who revives the dead,
Your power saves.
From heaven's well
send us water.

Grant us water;
for a blessing,
not for a curse.

Water for life,
not for death.

Water for plenty,
not for flood.

Oh Mighty Spirit who revives the dead,
do not refuse us in our dry times.
Remember the tribes
and grant us abundant water.

Find Me an Island

Find me an island
upstream from a sharp bend
on a winding staircase to the sea.

May it be washed by waters from Red Rock Creek,
from the Gates of the Mountains
and Great Falls, from the junction of the Yellowstone.

May the peoples who drank from its stream
give their names to myth. May they be called
Sans Arcs and Blackfeet, Minneconjous and Cheyenne,
Pawnee and Osage.

Find me a place of willows
and red cedar, rich with plums and bull berries,
haws and hackberries, bitter-root and wild onions,
where Indian turnips lurk in the buffalo grass.

I shall turn philosopher on such an island,
sure as Handsome Lake
I have found the way
it should be in our minds.

From the smooth sumac leaves
and the inner bark of the red willow,
from the leaves and bark of bear berry,
we shall make kinnikinnik. Breathe in.
Pass the pipe and breathe in the world.

Cow Island, November 1818

PATRICK: It's cold. Cold and frosty. This morning's warmth only teased us. Soon it will be too cold to put a man into his grave.

CRAFT: It's November already. What did you think it would come to in November?

PATRICK: A man's got a right to damn the weather. More than that, who knows who'll be kneeling by the river come spring.

CRAFT: We'll be warm enough. This day the officers began to issue blankets and such. We'll have warm winter clothing. Enough to survive.

PATRICK: Winter on Cow Island. Damnation, I can think of better places to survive.

CRAFT: I never called it St. Louis. It's not that. Captain Martin says we must be on our guard. Just yesterday two hunters returned empty handed. They say they killed six deer, but they returned with none.

PATRICK: Good venison left lying in the brush. It's a sin to leave venison to rot, especially with winter coming in. It's cold as Satan's hindquarters.

CRAFT: Oh they got the venison. The captain sent Dr. Gale in the *General Smith* with a party of twenty-five men to fetch it.

PATRICK: Twenty-five men?

The prisoners, members of the tribe known as Kansas, are charged 1st with THEFT, with stealing both public and private property from the Garrison, while permitted to encamp near it. Thus they repayed our hospitality and civilities with ingratitude and insult.

These same prisoners are charged 2nd, with HAVING ROBBED AND PLUNDERED our hunters of their game, ammunition, and wearing apparel, thereby breaking those holy bonds of amity and friendship they are pledged to observe. Thus they prove themselves false, treacherous, and dishonorable, unworthy of either our confidence or our protection.

(The CHIEF rises, looks over the soldiers, his captors, and addresses the Commanding Officer.)

CHIEF: Sir, You Who Would Be Honored,
your young men are prescribed within certain bounds.
Without your permission not one of them may pass
that chain of sentinels. They are always within your power,
and therefore governed with ease.
Not so my warriors. Not so.
Impatient as the wild horse,
they brook no control.
Free as the air they breathe,
light and impetuous as the antelope,
they sweep over plains, prairie and mountain.
They pursue nature, and what nature has ordained
is theirs to enjoy.
Who can confine them to one valley?
If one would deprive them of their subsistence,
they would shrivel and die,
like grasses along a dry creekbed.
These woods and streams are ours.
The beavers that inhabit this river
and the Buffalo that range in this land
are ours. Their skins afford us clothing
and shelter. The substance of their bodies
we change into ours.

Should we, who are children of earth,
quit the joys of tracking,
the necessary hunt, to become
like you, confined
to one valley,
practicing subordination and discipline,
living in indolence and idleness?

Sir, You Who Would Be Honored,
must understand. It cannot be so.
We will inhale the morning's breeze
on the mountain, in pursuit of the antelope.
By starlight we shall revel in the spoils
of our hunters and the caresses of our women.

Sir, You Who Would Be Honored,
we invite you to learn, to participate,
to take meat from the forest,
fish from the mountains.
We offer you an equal portion as ourselves,
freely as the Great Spirit gave them to us.

Sir, You Who Would Be Honored,
we respect you, offer our friendship.
We grieve that there are among us
those who have done wrong.
We grieve that you believe among us also
those who have harmed you.
If so, they were not within my control.
Punish not the innocent for the guilty.
Free our hands from these shackles.

If there are culprits among us,
we who are innocent will seek them out.
Though the evil crouch in the thickest tangle
or lie in caves of the most difficult mountain,
they shall be found out.

Sir, You Who Would Be Honored,
if those who have harmed you without cause
are among us, we shall surrender them
so that they may be corrected.
But punish not the innocent for the guilty.
Free our hands from these shackles.

CAPT. MARTIN: Mr. Rogers, what is your response?

ROGERS: Sophistry. Pure and simple sophistry from a savage. And what is more, lies. My men have pointed out five of the culprits, clearly seen by moonlight as the offenders.

CAPT. MARTIN: They shall be strongly enjoined to mend their manners and their morals.

ROGERS: Sir, let me recommend the appropriate punishment. The culprits we have recognized deserve severe flagellation. Whip them raw and throw them into the stream. The matter should then rightly be resolved.

CAPT. MARTIN: Sir, it shall be so. Lt. Field, consider that an order. Only when the rod of correction is wielded with authority shall proper control be established and we be worthy of the confidence of those for whom we bear responsibility.

Finis

Color Photos
by
Bob Barrett

Figure Found in a Group Photograph
of the Missouri Historical Society

Chin admirably cleft,
lips thin as reeds
& carefully closed,
Mr. Benjamin O Fallon
arrived downstream
from Council Bluffs
after conversations
with the Otoes & the Omaha.
Mr. O Fallon was concerned:
A half-breed had encouraged
less enlightened Indians
to "rise against the Agent."

Promptly O Fallon
ordered the offender
lashed, both his ears
cut off, his weapons
dumped into the river.
Then, to show his generosity,
Fallon set the fellow loose.

Mr. Benjamin O Fallon
was austerely handsome
& sure to find his place in history.
You may see him here
in all his finery.

Fermentation Time

He hikes by the Platte,
spits into the stream.
The land is slowly warming
into spring:
A contemplative bass
strokes a rounded rock;
they are companions,
absorbing the sun.

Two bald eagles
roost on a cottonwood
for an hour's thought
about the island
or the river
or just about
being half-way out.

He feels a poem
growing somewhere.

Weather Watch

Along the banks of the Little Blue
maples wrestle in the wind
under an introspective sky.

A weasel wanders warily through;
a deer accuses the midnight moon,
and the philosophic grasses sigh.

Slowly a pebble turns in its bed;
a squirrel assays the year's accounts;
a feather whispers to the stones.

While clouds convene to praise the dead,
tornadoes rant like oracles.
The roots are muttering, and the bones.

A Cardinal Flew Out of Missouri

A cardinal flew out of Missouri,
crossed the state line into Kansas,
paused high in an elm on Indian Creek.

The winter water iced along the edges,
glazed across the back of a whitetail fawn
curled into the creek bed, its neck broken.

The cardinal shifted its perch to a peeling poplar,
let go an almost imperceptible song,
like a string of bubbles in the shadows under a bridge.

Mist lifted up from the water, over the fawn,
over the bridge, back toward Missouri. The cardinal
flew off like an errant note, deep into Kansas.

River Behind the City

The river shapes the land,
hollows out pastures for repose,
feeds green to foliage,
cycles hydroplankton to humming wings.
Put your hand in the water.
Feel its downward tug.
From this spot, look west,
to the Missouri, to the Kaw.
You breathe in wanderings,
the chants of itinerant gods.

But look again:

By the Inter-City Viaduct,
at the first big bend east of Montana,
near where Kaw & Missouri become one,
two boys on bikes swoop along the levee.
Tractor trailors plunge under overpasses.
The stolid barges stubbornly advance.

Here, on Barrett's Beach,
you and the Brown Headed Cowbird
watch vapor trails tease the highest city hall around;
you stand beside the Big Muddy
wrested from its past,
pouring over itself,
a downstream rush, through
the Fairfax Industrial District, under
the Broadway Bridge. Yes, the Big
Muddy's gone, gone
with the Prairie Schooners,
gone with the Conestogas.
They are all wrapped up in the plans
of the Army Corps of Engineers.

Beware the muscular currents
of this new river. Men with machines
have aimed it,
tuned it to speed,
till it's one of the fastest,
urgent as the time.

Soaking Up the West in '76

One last sip in the River Quay
and we push off the foot of Grand
upstream into May,
a hundred tourists high on bourbon
and history, ready to soak up the West
in Seventy-Six.

We lounge and lean.
You shield your eyes like a scout
as the sun hints danger
to the North
pulsing purple and gold
through the refinery haze.
The Bicentennial tinder box is lit.
We're sucking up its energy.

We're all aboard
the *Westport Landing*
of the K.C. Excursion Boat Co.,
headed toward sky-country,

for a few minutes tuned
to pioneer dreams
by a paid guitarist
on the barge behind us.

"Up there," says the stuttering speaker,
"the scenic drama's over your head,
not under your feet."
And we believe, thinking,
"We're riding the river;
the pulse of the continent
is rubbing our hull."

So we celebrate,
gazing at water and shoreline,
proclaiming the heavens,
leaving behind us new trails
to follow, our wake a flotilla
of bobbing plastic cups.

On the Paseo Bridge
On the Chouteau Bridge

On the Paseo Bridge
the bodies of lovers
touch goodbye.
They part
like the hands of a clock
at noon or midnight.

On the Chouteau Bridge
the fisherman forgets his line.
He is too busy looking
for himself in the water.

Rivers make us young or old.
Their currents run across our foreheads.
We are right to be lonely
on the Paseo Bridge,
on the Chouteau Bridge.

Look down & conjure the tide.
The river below belongs to you.
Somewhere at bottom
you may see yourself
pulsing like a star.

On Barrett's Beach

what floats by likely washes up
according to the current,
the wind,   the water level,
the drag,   the eddy near the sandbar,
the season.
you can wait on Barrett's Beach
without a line or net
and collect surprises:
Bottles in branches,   scarlet birds
perched on crates of perilous apples.
if you could wait,   breathing through a reed,
slowly as a fern,
if you could let your wristwatch rust,
if you had the patience of feldspar,
all things would come to you here:
Hardware and crockery, truck tires
and 2 by 4's, transformed,
shaped by the depths,   sanded
and stroked into sculpture
for a landscape that will change
as the seasons of the river change.
the river slaps the bank.
a blue racer shudders through the brush;
a hawk catapults into the mist.
if you could wait long enough
you might watch all things
fade into water and air

One Leaf

One leaf,
like a small echo,
travels under cumulus
in an eastward spiral,
a downward curl
under curving branches
letting go their rafts of wings,
miniature clouds
that slowly grow heavy
and settle into the mud
that will not stay still
but subtly tilts and slides,
quietly wrestles
through eons
of accumulating weight
while the channel
twists back on itself
like a drifting leaf caught
in a sudden updraft before
it lights on the river's surface,
a beaded glint
of momentary green.
The river is more than water
or tides or silt or a graph
of direction, more than
a treelike confluence
with a mouth. Its weight
shifts eastward and southward;
and as it moves
its slow length along,
the earth arches
and the limestone shudders,
dissolving into great caves
in which bats flutter
swirling upward
in dark currents toward the surface.

More Than Two Hundred Years

More than two hundred years
we searched for a hidden Eden
Kings had overlooked,
for somewhere our madness could flower properly
away from the gardener's rusting shears,
where a Pole could dance his way to weariness,
Irish potatoes swell to pumpkin magnitude,
where a Jew could finger the fringes of his prayer shawl.

But a voice cried out:
      GIVE ME land, GIVE ME gold, GIVE ME cotton.
      GIVE ME the right of way.
      GIVE ME herds for my pleasure,
      and pelts, GIVE ME pelts.
      There are never enough.
      I am never sufficiently warm.
      So give me MORE, give me MORE.

      Nor is the new enough.
      So again GIVE ME the old.
      GIVE ME the old again.
      Build for me.
      Load antiques on the backs of coolies.
      Tapestry the shoulders of slaves.
      Call the serf a freeman and mortgage him under.
      There's no end here to possibilities.

But by night
the bearers slip away,
                the coolies, the slaves,
                            the helpless, the amazed.

Behind the Pioneer corn,
behind the Douglas fir,
under the culverts,
on the backside of the rotting cities,
their guises change.

WHO IS LOST?
AND WHO IS LOOKING FOR A PLACE?

Who can make out those shadows in the underbrush?
Whose voices jostle us on the intercoms?

The Nation Builder has plotted his tract.
He is plumbing hard
for the fountain of youth.
For title to the Elysian Fields.

Let's photograph his new development.
Ah, there's color richer than reality,
a TV Bird of Paradise,
a rainbow without haze,
carefully framed,
a rainbow like no other.
Look how it floats
upon the waters,
rainbow trails upon the water,
a swirl of irridescence near the wharves,
a shimmer of gasoline across the playground.

Ah, so rich and varied are these possibilities.

But who will give
and who will take?

While new developers survey the skies,
plan planetary subdivisions and ordinances,
draft azimuths and timetables
toward Alpha Centauri,
across the plains and prairies,
COYOTE is backtracking.
Behind the bunch grass and the corrugated sheds,
someone is looking for water
with a hazel wand.

There's still no ending here to possibility.

So Tom Benton knew,
on even his last trips,
stiff in the boat,
the fluid dry in his sockets.
Floating the Buffalo, the Current,
those limber rivers,
hearing the hounds yelping uneasily
for the marrow of the land,
he admitted no end to possibility.

Pick up that cup
from a rock glittering with spray
& kneel again
by the river.

Well

While the solar wind
powers the chariot of Apollo,
ordinary gusts course the Cascades
and the Rockies. Below,
along the Great Divide,
a system of membranes and capillaries
collects itself into a river
predictable as weather.

The river is a promise,
curling like the rainbows
that arch across it;

& we are thirsty for a clear potion,
a tankard of sunlight and chlorophyll,
a swig of Genesis,
a draft of the old rain
that shimmers in the cup
without isotopes or acid.

But now one needs a set of filters
to savor the air or the water,
to measure the flux.
Along the banks cities rust
and probe the currents
with pipes of excrement.
The great collector catfish
floats on its back,
clogged with cells.

    A bed of sediment
           older than man,
    saturated as if ice sheets
    were still melting into the ancestral flow,
    rests beneath the watercourse
           we call Missouri.

I drill a well into the Pleistocene,
    wonder if some medicine of the gods
        will bubble up for us to drink.

All the Seasons Pour into One River

All the seasons pour into one river,
summer sun slowly bobbing under the ice,
still glinting, emerging into spring.
Through the seasons we grow high, heavy,
half-way down drifting, till we're still
as cold rock, stiff, dried weeds,
aching for warmth, till feeling
returns, till pain spreads through fingertips
up through tendrils, till return
returns and the eyes lift and moist mornings
gently flower into branches of forsythia
floating on water.

All the seasons pour into one river,
summer sun slowly bobbing under the ice,
still glinting, emerging into spring,
and a poet's question coils in its eddies:
If what heals can bless, can what blesses heal?
But even as the Sears Tower sticks its steel index
finger into the apex,
Cheyenne and mountain man follow the chill pointer
onto the highway that weaves between the stars,
tracking the Bear through the heavens
until they ride the comet's tail, like Halley,
home, facing each other across the stream
as the snows melt and the water rises.

So green comes green again. And all the seasons
pour into one river,
summer sun slowly bobbing under the ice,
still glinting, emerging into spring.

NOTES

From the Great Bend

The Missouri River travels generally southeastward from Montana and almost due south into Missouri. When it reaches the Kansas River, it veers sharply to the east. The city of Kansas City is located at this "Great Bend of the Missouri."

The Map Is Not the River

Geographers generally classify rivers by length rather than breadth. Its length and the area drained by it and its tributaries make the Missouri River the continent's great river.

The Water Prayer

"The Water Prayer" is a fairly close adaptation of a tribal prayer devised by a 13th century Palestinian rabbi. It is chanted in Jewish synagogues each year during the festival of Succoth.

Find Me an Island

Handsome Lake, the Native American (Iroquois) philosopher, may be best remembered for "The Code of Handsome Lake," which contains the refrain: "This is the way it should be in our minds."

"Find Me an Island" contains the recipe for kinnikinnik, the substance smoked during rituals by many plains Indians. Often it was mixed with white man's tobacco.

Barrett's Beach

Barrett's Beach refers to the strip of land behind Kansas City's downtown Municipal Airport, directly east and across from the mouth of the Kansas (Kaw) River. It changes in size and shape according to water level and condition of the river. It is named after the photographer whose work appears in this book.

One Leaf

"One Leaf" refers to a theory held by a few geologists who hypothesize that over eons so much material moved down the Missouri that an additional burden beyond a critical point caused stone formations to buckle and create Missouri's great caves. Most scientists believe the caves result from the dissolution of limestone by water.

Well

The ancient Missouri River, in existence during the Pleistocene Era, may still be located in places under the watercourse of the present river. Water may be pumped up from deep down in the soaked sediment as if from an underground stream. Some believe in the purity of this source so close to early origins, but there is evidence of some mixing from surface waters.

All the Seasons Pour Into One River

In his poem "Come Green Again," Winfield Townley Scott asks the question posed in "All the Seasons Pour Into One River."

Dan Jaffe has written and edited books about the American West, including *Dan Freeman*, the biography of the first homesteader, in poetry and prose, illustrated by the Nebraska painter Aaron G. Pyle. Jaffe has written a jazz opera, a sequence of poems for chorale, and a number of plays as well as numerous essays about poets and poetry. Winner of a major Hopwood Prize at the University of Michigan, Jaffe has edited three anthologies of poems by young people. He is director of the Missouri Valley Writers Conference. His poems appear in many anthologies in the U.S., Australia, and New Zealand.

Bob Barrett's photographs have appeared widely. Readers of *National Geographic, Audubon, National Wildlife,* Time-Life Books*, New Letters* and many other publications have seen his work. He has had a number of one-man shows including "Portraits of Famous Kansas City Artists." He has documented Kansas City Art Deco architecture in photos. Barrett is a former staff photographer at the University of Missouri-Kansas City. Currently, he operates his own studio. He does commercial and industrial photography, but his special concerns are naturalism and ecology. A friend of the late Thomas Hart Benton, Barrett photographed Benton and helped Benton on his last mural.

Lydia Swartz is a native of Kansas City where she has operated an art gallery and worked as a photographer. She is a student in Baker University's Master of Liberal Arts program and has done post-graduate work at UMKC. She has traveled extensively in Asia and currently lives in the Philippines with her husband Jack.

OTHER BOOKS FROM BkMk PRESS

Tanks, short fiction by John Mort. "Chilling glimpses of the Vietnam War. These are terrifying, but sensitive stories." —Bobbie Ann Mason. $8.95

Missouri Short Fiction, edited by Conger Beasley, Jr. Twenty-three short stories by Missouri writers including Bob Shacochis, Speer Morgan, James McKinley, John Mort, Charles Hammer, David Ray and others. $8.95

Voices from the Interior, edited by Robert Stewart. Poems by over 50 of Missouri's finest poets. $6.50

Modern Interiors, by Stephen Gosnell. Quality lithographic reproductions with short interrelated fictional pieces. $12.95

Selected Poems of Mbembe Milton Smith. "One of our most nourishing poets... He used language deftly with lively, affectionate respect." —Gwendolyn Brooks. $8.95

Artificial Horizon, by Laurence Gonzales. "...a first rate young writer whose work merits attention from anyone seeking lively idiom, authentic detail and a fresh point of view..." —Edward Abbey. $8.95

In the Middle: Midwestern Women Poets, edited by Sylvia Wheeler. Poems & essays by Lisel Mueller, Faye Kicknosway, Joan Yeagley, Diane Hueter, Sonia Gernes, Janet Beeler Shaw, Roberta Hill Whiteman, Dorothy Selz & Cary Waterman. $9.50

Dark Fire, by Bruce Cutler. A book-length narrative poem, "...a lively, imaginative, and finely crafted tale of modern life." —Judson Jerome in Writer's Digest. $6.25

Wild Bouquet, by Harry Martinson. The first American collection of these nature poems by the Swedish Nobel Laureate. Translated and with an introduction by William Jay Smith and Leif Sjöberg. $10.95 cloth

Writing in Winter, by Constance Scheerer. "...one of the fresher voices out of the Midwest...vivid and memorable." —David Ray $5.25

Hi-Fi & The False Bottom, by Goran Stefanovski. Two plays by a well-known Yugoslavian playwright, translated from the original Macedonian. Introduction by James McKinley. $8.50

The Record-Breaking Heatwave, poems by Jeff Friedman. "This is urban poetry, working class poetry, strongly felt, carefully observed, cleanly written..." —Donald Justice. $8.00 cloth

The Eye of the Ghost: Vietnam Poems, by Bill Bauer. "Bill Bauer takes us well into the experience of Vietnam with a sure sense of the catastrophe that war proved for those who were involved. These poems demonstrate not only craft and dedication to the poet's art, but also an abiding commitment to justice and compassion." —Bruce Cutler. $8.00 cloth